The American Civil War

BY
CINDY BARDEN

COPYRIGHT © 2002 Mark Twain Media, Inc.

ISBN 1-58037-186-8

Printing No. CD-1532

Mark Twain Media, Inc., Publishers
Distributed by Carson-Dellosa Publishing Company, Inc.

Table of Contents

About the American History Series

Welcome to *The American Civil War*, one of the books in the Mark Twain Media, Inc., American History series for students in grades four to seven.

The activity books in this series are designed as stand-alone material for classrooms and home-schoolers or as supplemental material to enhance your history curriculum. Students can be encouraged to use the books as independent study units to improve their understanding of historical events and people.

Each book provides challenging activities that enable students to explore history, geography, and social studies topics. The activities provide research opportunities and promote critical reading, thinking, and writing skills. As students learn about the people and events that influenced history, they will draw conclusions; write opinions; compare and contrast historical events, people, and places; analyze cause and effect; and improve mapping skills. Students will also have the opportunity to apply what they learn to their own lives through reflection and creative writing.

Students can further increase their knowledge and understanding of historical events by using reference sources at the library and on the Internet. Students may need assistance to learn how to use search engines and discover appropriate websites.

Titles of books for additional reading appropriate to the subject matter at this grade level are included in each book.

Although many of the questions are open-ended, answer keys are included at the back of the book for questions with specific answers.

Share a journey through history with your students as you explore the books in the Mark Twain Media, Inc., American History series:

Discovering and Exploring the Americas
Life in the Colonies
The American Revolution
The Lewis and Clark Expedition
The Westward Movement
The California Gold Rush
The Oregon and Santa Fe Trails
Slavery in the United States
The American Civil War
Abraham Lincoln and His Times
The Reconstruction Era
Industrialization in America
The Roaring Twenties and Great Depression
World War II and the Post-War Years
America in the 1960s and 1970s
America in the 1980s and 1990s

Time Line of *The American Civil War*

1619   The first slaves were brought to Jamestown colony by a Dutch trader.

1688   The first formal protest of slavery in the Americas was signed by Pennsylvania Quakers.

1776   The Declaration of Independence was signed.

1786   Importation of new slaves ended in all states except Georgia and South Carolina.

1787   Slavery was prohibited in the Northwest Territory.

1793   The first federal Fugitive Slave Act made it illegal to assist runaway slaves.

1807   British Parliament prohibited British subjects from engaging in the slave trade after March 1, 1808.

1820   The Missouri Compromise was put into effect.

1850   The second Fugitive Slave Law was passed.

1852   *Uncle Tom's Cabin* was published.

1857   The Supreme Court ruled in the *Dred Scott* case.

1860   **November:** Abraham Lincoln was elected president.
       December: South Carolina seceded from the Union.

1861   **January:** Mississippi, Florida, Alabama, Georgia, and Louisiana seceded from the Union.
       January 29: Kansas was admitted to the Union.
       February 1: Texas seceded from the Union.
       February 9: Jefferson Davis was elected President of the Confederate States of America.
       March 4: Abraham Lincoln was inaugurated as president.
       April 12: The Battle at Fort Sumter began.
       April 17: Virginia seceded from the Union.
       May: Arkansas, Tennessee, and North Carolina seceded from the Union.
       July 21: The First Battle of Bull Run was fought.
       November: George McClellan was appointed head of the Union Army.
                Richmond, Virginia, was named the Confederate capital.

Time Line of *The American Civil War*

1862   **March 9:** The battle between the U.S.S. *Monitor* and the C.S.S. *Virginia (Merrimac)* took place.

April 6–7: The Battle of Shiloh was fought.

June: Robert E. Lee was appointed commander of the Army of Northern Virginia.

June 25–July 1: The Battle of the Seven Days was fought.

August 29–30: The Second Battle of Bull Run was fought.

September 17: The Battle of Antietam was fought.

November 7: Ambrose Burnside replaced McClellan.

December 13: The Battle of Fredericksburg was fought.

1863   **January 1:** Lincoln issued the Emancipation Proclamation.

January 26: Joseph Hooker replaced Burnside.

March: The first Conscription Act was passed.

May 1–4: The Battle of Chancellorsville was fought.

May 22: The siege of Vicksburg began.

June 19: West Virginia joined the Union as a separate state.

June 28: George Meade replaced Hooker.

July 1–3: The Battle of Gettysburg was fought.

July 4: The Confederate fort at Vicksburg was surrendered to Union General Ulysses Grant.

November 19: Lincoln delivered his Gettysburg Address.

1864   **March 12:** Ulysses S. Grant became supreme commander of the Union Army.

June 1–3: The Battle of Cold Harbor was fought.

July 22: The Battle of Atlanta was fought.

September: Union troops occupied Atlanta.

November 8: President Lincoln was reelected.

November 15: William T. Sherman began his march to the sea from Atlanta to Savannah.

1865   **March 4:** Lincoln began his second term as president.

April 3: The Union Army captured Richmond.

April 9: The Civil War ended when General Lee surrendered.

April 14: President Lincoln was assassinated.

April 15: Andrew Johnson became president.

December 6: The Thirteenth Amendment abolished slavery.

Name: _____ Date: _____

What Caused the Civil War?

What caused the Civil War? The most common answer is slavery. There is no doubt that the disagreement about slavery was a major cause. Although there were many differences between the Southern and Northern states, slavery was the only institution not shared by both areas.

Not only did they disagree about the legality and morality of slavery, but they also disagreed about extending slavery into the West. Northerners wanted to end the expansion of slavery into new territories. Slave owners wanted to extend slavery to all new states.

Another major issue was states' rights. Southerners believed individual states should have more control over laws than the federal government.

The North and South disagreed on tariffs (taxes on goods brought in from another country). As early as the 1830s, South Carolina threatened to leave the Union over this issue. Farmers and plantation owners of the South wanted to sell their cotton and tobacco to other countries and buy manufactured goods as cheaply as possible because the South had few factories.

Northern factory owners wanted high tariffs on imported goods so they could sell their own products in the United States. They wanted to keep out competition by making foreign goods more expensive.

In 1860, a lawyer in Georgia stated: "... in this country have arisen two races [Northerners and Southerners] which ... have been so entirely separated by climate, by morals, by religion, and by estimates so totally opposite to all that constitutes honor, truth, and manliness, that they cannot exist under the same government."

Use the Internet and other reference sources to learn more about an issue other than slavery that contributed to the secession of the Southern states and the outbreak of the Civil War. On your own paper, summarize the views of the North and the South on that issue.

SLAVE STATE   FREE STATE

4

Name: _____ Date: _____

An Overview of Slavery

Slavery did not begin when the first Dutch ship traded a cargo of African slaves for food at the Jamestown colony in 1619. Nor did it end when slavery was outlawed in the United States in 1865. Slavery has been a part of human history since the earliest times.

People in ancient China, Mesopotamia, India, Egypt, Greece, and Rome owned slaves. In South America, the Aztecs, Incas, and Mayas practiced slavery. Being a slave meant being forced to work without any pay or benefits.

Some people became slaves as a form of punishment because they committed crimes or couldn't pay their debts. The term of slavery was set for a period of years. After that time, they were again free. Their children usually remained free.

In 1441 a Portuguese trader kidnapped ten Africans and took them to Portugal as slaves. Kidnapping as a way of obtaining slaves continued for a time, but this soon led to conflict with African leaders. Rather than kidnapping, Portuguese traders could exchange horses, silks, and silver for slaves. Slavery was common in Africa at the time. Most slaves were prisoners of war who became slaves for life. Their children automatically became slaves.

The African leaders were willing to trade slaves for goods with Europeans. Spain, Portugal, the Netherlands, and other European countries traded goods for slaves with the rulers of several great empires (Mali, Benin, Dahomey, and Kongo) along the coast of Africa.

By 1448 there were about 1,000 slaves in Portugal, mainly used for agricultural work. The Spanish imported slaves to work in their colonies in the New World. Dutch traders took the first slaves to the British colony of Jamestown in 1619.

Although slavery is illegal in all countries today, people are still forced into conditions very much like slavery in some countries.

1. How would you feel about being a slave? Be specific.

    _____

    _____

    _____

    _____

2. On your own paper, explain what you think of slavery as a form of punishment for crimes.

5

Name: _____ Date: _____

What Rights Did Slaves Have?

Each colony enacted its own laws regarding slavery, but by the 1680s, the laws in most colonies were similar. Slavery was legal in all colonies. Slaves were not recognized as persons by law; therefore, they had no legal rights.

Slavery was a permanent condition inherited through the mother. Slaves were considered property. They could be bought, sold, punished, or loaned to someone else, the same way a person might loan a neighbor a hoe or a horse. Like other forms of property, slaves could be passed on to others in a will or given away.

Slaves could not own any property, make contracts, serve as witnesses in a court, or serve on juries. Since marriage is a contract, no slave marriage was considered legal.

Even freed slaves were restricted by laws that controlled their travel, employment, and legal status. In many states, a freed slave was required to leave the state.

Slaves charged with crimes in Virginia were tried in a special court. They had no rights to trial by jury. The purpose of the trial was not to seek justice, but to set an example for other slaves by imposing terrible punishments that could include whipping, branding, or a tortured death.

Slaves could be bought and sold at auction as if they were property.

1. What rights do you think your skates or TV have? _____

2. What rights do you think pets or other animals have? _____

3. How would you feel if you were considered the property of another person?

   _____

   _____

   _____

4. Do you think slaves were treated more like objects or animals? Explain your answer.

   _____

   _____

   _____

5. On your own paper, write down what you think your most important right is. Why?

Name: _____ Date: _____

Not All Southerners Were Slaveholders

Most people think of White Southerners in the 1700s and 1800s as slave owners, but only one in four Southern families actually owned slaves. Three-quarters of Southern families did not own slaves.

By the time the Civil War began in 1861, about 25 percent of the Blacks in the South were free. Most free Blacks in the South weren't much better off than slaves, but in some areas they were allowed to marry, own property, attend schools, and even own slaves of their own.

Eli Whitney

Not all slaves worked on huge plantations. Only about 30,000 Southerners owned fifty or more slaves. Most Southerners who owned slaves lived and worked on smaller farms and in cities. Slaves also worked in shipyards, in businesses, and as house slaves.

Sometimes slaves were hired out by their masters and all wages were paid to their owners. Southerners needed cheap labor to work the fields of cotton and tobacco. This made slavery very important to the economy.

The invention of the cotton gin by Eli Whitney in 1793 cut the cost of producing cotton. This machine could clean cotton much faster than people could. Since this lowered the cost of

producing cotton, the price went down, and the demand for cotton cloth increased. Growing more cotton meant the need for even more workers.

Wealthy families who owned large plantations and many slaves wanted to maintain their status by controlling the source of their wealth—cotton, slaves, and all laws regarding slavery. Unlike other societies, slavery in the South was not based on forcing prisoners of war to be slaves—slavery was based on race.

The early European colonists believed that Africans were inferior, suited by their character and circumstances to be slaves forever. This attitude remained most strongly in the South, long after Europe abolished slavery and the slave trade.

1. What percentage of Southerners were not slaveholders? _____

2. How would you feel if you were forced to go to work six days a week for ten or more hours a day, but received no pay for your work?

   _____

   _____

3. How would you feel if you were a farmer today and the government wanted to pass a law making tractors illegal?

   _____

   _____

Name: _____ Date: _____

Northerners Had Slaves Too

The attitude towards slavery in the North was very mixed. Not every Northerner believed slaves should be free. Even among those who wanted to abolish slavery, many didn't think Blacks deserved equal rights.

Slavery was common in all the Northern American colonies for a time. The Dutch in New Amsterdam imported slaves to work on their farms in the Hudson Valley. According to Dutch law, children of freed slaves were still legally slaves.

Other Europeans who settled in the New World kept slaves to work in their homes, on farms, and in businesses. Most shipowners and sea captains involved in the slave trade were Northerners. Several Northern coastal cities became centers for slave traffic. Slavery existed in every American colony until the Revolutionary War. Vermont was the first to end slavery in 1777. New York was the last Northern state to abolish slavery in 1817.

Even after slavery became illegal in the North, the lives of free Blacks living there were very difficult. Whites, especially recent immigrants, feared Blacks would take over jobs, leaving them unemployed. Mobs rampaged through areas where Blacks lived and worked in Ohio and New York. Many Blacks fled to Canada.

White rioters in Philadelphia in 1834 and 1842 destroyed Black churches, attacked Black men and women on the streets, and burned their homes. In some states, federal troops were needed to stop the violence.

Schools that allowed Black students to attend were destroyed in several Northern states. In Canterbury, Connecticut, shop owners refused to sell supplies to a woman who ran a private school that admitted Black girls; her neighbors even tried to poison her well. Finally, she was ordered to close the school and was arrested. The townspeople then destroyed the school building.

On your own paper, answer the following questions.

1. Imagine living in a large Northern city. Mobs of White people are rampaging through your city, attacking Blacks, and destroying their homes. What would you do?

2. If you were a White person living in Canterbury, Connecticut, how would you have felt about the woman who ran the school?

Name: _____ Date: _____

The Constitution: Many Compromises

After the Revolutionary War, the leaders of the new nation met to write a constitution. Although slavery was illegal in the Northern states, slavery was not abolished in the Constitution. If that had been part of the Constitution, delegates from the Southern states would have refused to sign, and the Southern states would have refused to ratify it.

The writers of the Constitution decided it was more important to put together a strong new nation than to deal with the difficult and controversial issue of slavery.

The Constitution stated that the federal government could not abolish the importation of new slaves for 20 years and gave slave owners the right to capture runaway slaves, even in states where slavery was illegal.

There were other issues besides slavery that needed to be solved. Many compromises were made before the final draft of the Constitution was approved.

Large states wanted more representatives in Congress, based on population. Small states wanted equal representation. In the Constitution, all states received equal representation in the Senate. The number of members of the House of Representatives was based on population. Although the Southern states refused to consider slaves as people, they wanted them included in their total population. This made another compromise necessary: for representation, each slave was counted as $\frac{3}{5}$ of a person.

States' rights were a major concern, primarily to Southerners who considered belonging to the United States as a voluntary agreement. They wanted to limit the powers of the federal government. They claimed each state could determine if a federal law was constitutional and could refuse to carry out federal laws if that law infringed on the state's rights.

1. Use a thesaurus. List five synonyms for *infringe.* _____

   _____

2. What is your opinion of the compromise of making each slave count for $\frac{3}{5}$ of a person?

   _____

   _____

   _____

3. Do you agree or disagree with the decision of the writers of the Constitution in not dealing with the issue of slavery? Explain your answer on your own paper.

Name: _____ Date: _____

The Federal Fugitive Slave Laws

People who have been forced into slavery have always sought ways to escape their bondage. In the United States, slaves from Southern states fled to Northern states or Canada where slavery was illegal. Southerners objected when slaves escaped because they lost "valuable property."

The federal fugitive slave laws in the United States made it easier for slave owners to return runaways to their homes, even if they were captured in a state where slavery was illegal. These laws reinforced the commitment of the federal government to the belief that slaves were property.

The Fugitive Slave Law of 1793 allowed slave owners or their agents to capture fugitives in any state or territory. Whites in Northern cities often tried to stop "slave-catchers," professional bounty hunters who hunted for, captured, and returned runaway slaves to their masters.

Northerners objected to the fugitive slave laws, because they felt the laws denied individual liberty. Many Northerners believed that once a slave entered a free state, he or she should automatically be free. They also felt the laws offered too little protection for freed slaves who were often kidnapped and sold back into slavery.

Slave owners felt the law wasn't strong enough. There were no penalties for helping a slave escape or harboring a fugitive. They believed the federal law violated the rights of states to make their own laws regarding property.

In 1850, the federal government passed a stricter fugitive slave law making it mandatory for federal marshals to assist in recapturing runaways. It also penalized anyone helping a slave escape; penalties included fines and imprisonment for up to six months.

1. With which side do you agree? Give reasons for your answers. _____

    _____

    _____

2. How do you think Northerners felt about the stricter fugitive slave law? _____

    _____

    _____

3. How do you think slave owners felt about the 1850 law? _____

    _____

    _____

Name: _____ Date: _____

Meet Harriet Beecher Stowe

When Harriet Beecher moved with her family to Cincinnati in 1832, she first learned about the realities of slavery, which was legal across the Ohio River in Kentucky. She talked to fugitive slaves, heard stories of cruelty, and learned of the separation of husbands from wives and parents from children. She read advertisements for the return of runaway slaves and saw slave-catchers at work.

Harriet Beecher Stowe

After marrying Reverend Calvin Stowe, Harriet moved with him to Maine. Although she had five children and a home to care for, Harriet helped support her family by writing newspaper and magazine articles.

When Congress passed the Fugitive Slave Act of 1850, Harriet's sister wrote to her: "If I could use a pen as you can, I would write something that will make this nation feel what an accursed thing slavery is." So, at her sister's suggestion, Harriet wrote a fictional story about slavery, which was published in 1851 and 1852 as a serial for an antislavery magazine. Harriet painted a vivid picture of what she had seen and heard about slavery. She wove her story around fictional characters and situations based on real people and experiences.

A short time later, *Uncle Tom's Cabin* was published as a book. Although the magazine articles did not receive much attention, the book was an immediate sensation. The first 5,000 copies sold out in two days. Another 20,000 copies sold in the next three weeks. The publisher couldn't keep up with the demand for copies in the United States and Europe.

Harriet's story enabled readers to see slaves as real people forced to live in an unjust and cruel situation. *Uncle Tom's Cabin* drew so much attention and was read by so many people, it may have been one factor that led to the Civil War.

1. If you were able to write a book that would influence people regarding a major issue today, what issue would you write about and why?

    _____

    _____

    _____

    _____

    _____

    _____

    _____

Name: _____ Date: _____

Traveling the Underground Railroad

In spite of the fugitive slave laws, slaves still tried to escape, and people helped them by running the Underground Railroad, a series of houses, caves, hay mounds, root cellars, attics, chimneys, hidden rooms, sheds, and barns—places where runaway slaves could hide for a short time. The Underground Railroad also referred to the paths and trails that led from one shelter to the next and to the people, White and Black, who helped lead slaves to freedom.

Most of the first guides on the Underground Railroad were slaves or former slaves. Freed slaves put themselves in danger of becoming imprisoned, killed, or enslaved again by helping runaways. Some slaves who had fled to freedom, like Harriet Tubman, returned to help friends and family members escape.

Since it was a secret organization, no one knows for sure how many people became part of the Underground Railroad. John Mason, Josiah Henson, J.W. Loguen, John Parker, and Harriet Tubman were among more than 500 Black "conductors" on the Underground Railroad. About 75,000 slaves escaped with the help of the courageous "conductors" on the Underground Railroad.

Along the route to freedom, runaways stayed in safe houses and secret hiding places where they could eat and rest before continuing their journeys.

Quakers—members of a religious group that strongly opposed slavery—were among the first Whites to join the Underground Railroad. Other Whites in both the North and South helped slaves escape. Although the Fugitive Slave Law of 1850 made it illegal to help runaway slaves, many people ignored the law.

Slave owners feared a major slave uprising and the escape of their slaves. Since a slave could be worth a lot of money, a slave who ran away meant an economic loss. They also knew that each slave who escaped encouraged others to try.

1. If you had escaped slavery, how do you think you would have felt about going back to rescue friends or family members?

   _____

   _____

   _____

2. Do you think it was right or wrong to break the fugitive slave laws? Why?

   _____

   _____

Name: _____ Date: _____

Abolitionists

Abolitionists were people who actively tried to end slavery. They agreed that slavery was wrong, but did not always agree on how to solve the problem. Some abolitionists believed they could convince others of the evils of slavery by publishing newspapers, almanacs, and books.

Abolitionist societies sponsored lectures and invited former slaves like Frederick Douglass and Sojourner Truth to speak at their meetings. They hoped that hearing about the horrors of slavery from former slaves would convince the audience to take action.

Sometimes, however, the audience responded to those who spoke out against slavery by throwing rotten eggs or rocks. Elijah Lovejoy, publisher of an abolitionist newspaper in Alton, Illinois, was killed by a proslavery mob.

In the 1840s, abolitionist societies used songs to stir up enthusiasm at their meetings. To make the songs easier to learn, new words were often set to familiar tunes.

Many abolitionists wanted to end slavery peacefully by legal means through religious and political pressure. By making people aware of the evils of slavery, they felt that the laws permitting slavery would be repealed.

Even among those who believed slavery was wrong, many did not think Blacks should have equal rights. They wanted Blacks to be free from slavery, but not free to attend the same schools and churches or live in the same neighborhoods. Their solution was to free all slaves and return them to Africa.

William Lloyd Garrison began publishing an antislavery newspaper, *The Liberator,* on January 1, 1831, and he helped form the American Anti-Slavery Society. Although slavery was legal, Garrison felt it was wrong. "That which is not just is not law," he wrote.

Garrison's newspaper differed from previous abolitionist publications because it labeled slave owners as criminals and called for immediate abolition.

Some abolitionists, like John Brown, believed violence was the only way to end slavery.

1. On another sheet of paper, state your opinion of what you think would have been the best way for abolitionists to end slavery. Include several reasons for your opinion.

13

Name: _____ Date: _____

Slave States or Free States?

Missouri applied for statehood in 1819 as a slave state (a state where slavery was legal). Many Northerners objected because there were 11 free states and 11 slave states. By adding another slave state, the balance of power in Congress would go to those who were proslavery, opening the door for even more slave states to be admitted. They wanted to completely stop the spread of slavery, even if they couldn't eliminate it in the South.

Southern congressmen felt that since the Constitution granted the right to own slaves, that right would be denied if Missouri became a free state because all slave owners in Missouri would lose their slaves. They felt it was the duty of the federal government to protect private property.

At that time, Maine was not a separate state; it was part of Massachusetts. Maine also applied for statehood. Southern congressman refused to allow Maine to enter the Union as a free state unless Missouri was allowed to enter as a slave state.

Finally in 1820, Congress passed the Missouri Compromise, which admitted Missouri as a slave state and Maine as a free state. In addition, a line was drawn through the Louisiana Purchase at the southern border of Missouri. North of that line, slavery was prohibited forever. Although the Missouri Compromise became a law in 1820, few people on either side of the slavery issue were happy about it.

In 1854 Congress passed the Kansas-Nebraska Act, which allowed inhabitants of each territory to decide for themselves whether they wanted to apply for statehood as a free state or slave state.

Violent battles between proslavery and antislavery settlers turned into a bloody war, especially in Kansas. Fighting continued for several years, extending the hard feelings that eventually led to the Civil War.

1. Would you have voted for the Missouri Compromise? Why or why not?

_____

_____

_____

_____

_____

2. What is your opinion of the Kansas-Nebraska Act? _____

_____

_____

_____

_____

Name: _____ Date: _____

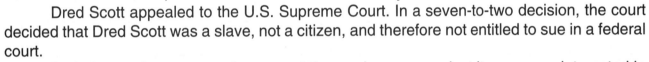

Meet Dred Scott

Dred Scott's owner, Peter Blow, moved to St. Louis in 1830 and sold him to Dr. John Emerson, an army surgeon. When Emerson went to Illinois, then to Fort Snelling, an army post in the Wisconsin Territory, he took his slave with him.

While at Fort Snelling, Dred Scott married another slave, Harriet Robinson. He and his wife remained at Fort Snelling after Emerson returned to St. Louis and then joined him in 1840.

When Dr. Emerson died, Dred Scott went to court to obtain freedom for himself, his wife, and their two daughters. He claimed that because they had lived in a free state and a free territory, they had been free, even though they had returned to a slave state. Once free, they should remain free.

Dred Scott was born a slave in Virginia about 1800. The decision made by the Supreme Court in the *Dred Scott* case may have been another factor that contributed to the Civil War.

The St. Louis Circuit Court agreed, but the Missouri Supreme Court reversed the decision, claiming that Missouri would not recognize any federal or state laws that freed slaves. Therefore, the Scotts were slaves and always had been.

Dred Scott appealed to the U.S. Supreme Court. In a seven-to-two decision, the court decided that Dred Scott was a slave, not a citizen, and therefore not entitled to sue in a federal court.

Both those who were proslavery and those who were against it were very interested in learning the outcome of this case.

Chief Justice Taney claimed Blacks were not and could never be U.S. citizens (even though free Black men were considered citizens and allowed to vote in several Northern states).

1. How do you think proslavery people felt about the outcome?

_____

_____

_____

_____

2. How do you think antislavery people felt about the decision?

_____

_____

_____

_____

Name: _____ Date: _____

Write All About It

The year is 1860. You have strong feelings about the evils of slavery and the rights of all people to "life, liberty, and the pursuit of happiness." Some people believe violence is the only way to end slavery. Others have suggested that the country be divided into two separate nations.

What do you think should be done? Write an editorial for your newspaper to convince others to see your point of view.

_____

_____

_____

_____

_____

_____

_____

_____

_____

_____

_____

_____

_____

_____

_____

_____

_____

_____

Name: _____ Date: _____

Tidbits of Civil War Trivia

- Grover Cleveland, who later became the President of the United States, avoided being drafted during the Civil War by paying a substitute to serve in his place.

- Shortly after the Civil War began, Abraham Lincoln asked Robert E. Lee to take command of the Union Army. Lee refused. He eventually became supreme commander of the Confederate Army.

- General Stonewall Jackson is buried in two places. His left arm was amputated after the battle of Chancellorsville and buried on a nearby farm. When he died a week later, Jackson was buried in Lexington, Virginia.

- General Ulysses S. Grant believed that onions prevented dysentery and other illnesses. He reportedly sent a message to the War Department refusing to move his army unless he had onions. A day later, the government sent him three trainloads of onions.

- General Robert E. Lee traveled with a hen during the Civil War so he could have fresh eggs for breakfast.

- Because of the shortage of coins, the U.S. Treasury Department printed paper money worth 1 cent, 5 cents, and 25 cents in 1862.

- The U.S. government used lotteries to raise money during the Civil War.

- News was sent by telegraph during the Civil War, but there was no telegraph office in the White House. President Lincoln had to walk across the street to the War Department to learn the news.

- Belle Boyd became a famous Confederate spy at age 17. She was finally captured near the end of the war. Her captor, Lt. Samuel Haringe, married her and left the U.S. Navy to join the Confederates.

- While a Congressman, Thomas Jefferson introduced a bill to bar slavery from all new states admitted to the Union. This may have prevented the Civil War, but it was defeated—by one vote.

- The Navy continued to use some of the ironclad ships built by the Union during the Civil War until 1926.

Belle Boyd was a Confederate spy.

- Too many chiefs? The Union Army had 2,537 generals!

1. Write two other interesting bits of Civil War trivia. _____

_____

_____

Name: _____   Date: _____

The Election of 1860

By 1860, the nation was divided on the issues of slavery and states' rights. The newly-formed Republican party nominated Abraham Lincoln as its candidate. Lincoln stated his views on slavery very clearly during his campaign. "I will not abolish slavery where it already exists, but we must not let the practice spread. I am opposed to allowing slavery in the new territories."

Although Lincoln's political rival, Stephen Douglas, was nominated as the Democratic candidate, conflict arose between the radical and conservative Democrats. A separate convention of radical Southern Democrats nominated their own candidate, John C. Breckenridge of Kentucky.

Another group, dedicated to keeping the country united, formed a new political party, the Constitutional Unionists, and nominated John Bell of Tennessee. With the Democratic party split between three candidates, it was doubtful that any of them could win.

To become president, one candidate needed at least 152 electoral votes. When the votes were counted, Lincoln had clearly won.

Candidate	Popular Votes	Electoral Votes
Abraham Lincoln	1,766,452	180
Stephen Douglas	1,376,957	12
John C. Breckenridge	849,781	72
John Bell	588,879	39

Lincoln won in all states in the North as well as in California and Oregon. Breckenridge won all states in the South, plus Maryland and Delaware. Bell won in Tennessee, Kentucky, and Virginia. Although Douglas had the second most popular votes, he only won in Missouri and part of New Jersey, giving him the lowest number of electoral votes.

In the 1800s many candidates had nicknames. Abe Lincoln was known as "the Railsplitter" and "Honest Abe." Stephen Douglas was nicknamed the "Little Giant."

1. Slogans and songs also helped voters identify with candidates. Write a campaign slogan for each of the candidates in the 1860 presidential campaign. Example: Honest Abe, he's our man. He'll hold us together if anyone can.

Lincoln _____

Douglas _____

Breckenridge _____

Bell _____

Name: _____   Date: _____

What Would You Do?

1. You live in South Carolina in 1860. Your friends, family, and neighbors have stated that if Abraham Lincoln is elected president, they will vote to secede. You believe secession may cause many problems, maybe even a war. What would you do?

    _____

    _____

    _____

2. The publisher of an antislavery newspaper has asked you to write an article for his newspaper. Many of the reporters for this newspaper have been attacked by angry mobs, beaten, and their homes were burned. What would you do?

    _____

    _____

    _____

3. You have learned about secret plans for a slave rebellion. You believe slavery is wrong, but you know that many innocent people may be killed if the rebellion takes place. What would you do?

    _____

    _____

    _____

4. You and your brother live in the South. You both agree that slavery is wrong. He has stated that if war begins, he will move to the North and join the Union Army. You feel it is your duty to stay and protect your family and property. What would you do?

    _____

    _____

    _____

5. You are a time traveler. You know that if Abraham Lincoln wins the election, many Southern states will secede from the Union, a war will begin, and thousands will die. What would you do?

    _____

    _____

    _____

Name: _____ Date: _____

Secession Divides the Nation: Part 1

When Abraham Lincoln was elected president in November 1860, there were 33 states in the Union. By the time he took office in March 1861, seven states had decided they no longer wanted to be a part of the United States.

South Carolina seceded from the United States in December 1860. The following year Alabama, Arkansas, Florida, Georgia, Louisiana, Mississippi, North Carolina, Tennessee, Texas, and Virginia joined South Carolina to form the Confederate States of America. They elected Jefferson Davis as their new president.

Their argument was that the Union was an organization of independent states. Since they chose to join it, they could also choose to leave it. When the North refused to accept their decision, the Southern states regarded the Civil War as a second war of independence.

When the Civil War began, slavery was legal in four border states: Delaware, Maryland, Kentucky, and Missouri. It was even legal in the nation's capital, Washington, D.C.

For a time, it was uncertain what would happen in the border states between the North and South. Although the South expected Kentucky and Missouri to join the Confederacy, in the end all four states remained with the Union. Kansas joined the Union as a state in January 1861, and part of Virginia separated from the rest of the state and became West Virginia, a Union state in 1863.

1. From the point of view of the South, why do you think the South considered the Civil War a war for independence?

    _____

    _____

    _____

    _____

    _____

    _____

2. From the point of view of the North, why do you think the North considered this a rebellion?

    _____

    _____

    _____

    _____

    _____

    _____

Name: _____ Date: _____

Secession Divides the Nation: Part 2

Use an atlas and the information on the previous page to complete this activity.

1. Color the Confederate states grey.

2. Color the states blue that did not secede.

3. The section called Indian Territory later became what state? _____

4. Name the other seven U.S. territories shown on the map. _____

    _____

    _____

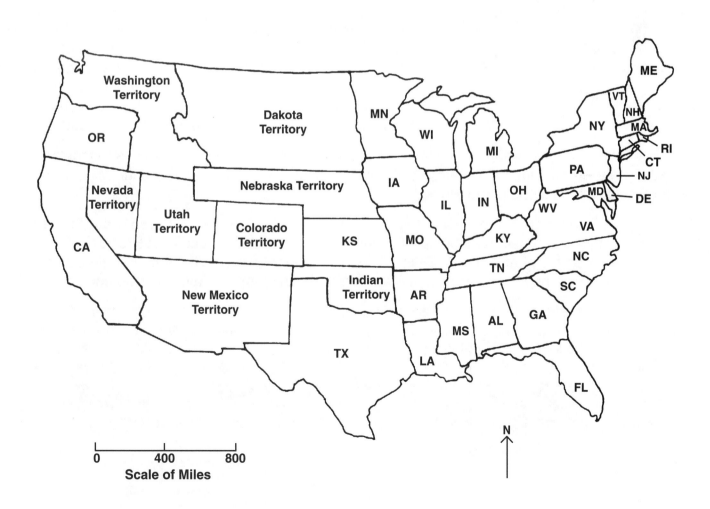

Meet Jefferson Davis

The youngest of ten children, Jefferson Davis was born in Kentucky in 1808 and moved with his family to Mississippi two years later. His father, a farmer, worked along with his slaves to clear the land and plant cotton.

Davis attended Transylvania University in Kentucky and the U.S. Military Academy at West Point. He graduated 23rd of 32 in 1828. Davis served at frontier outposts in the Wisconsin and Michigan Territories. There, he met and fell in love with Sarah Knox Taylor, the daughter of Zachary Taylor.

After their marriage in June 1835, Davis resigned his army commission and moved to Mississippi. His wife died of malaria three months after their wedding.

Davis married 19-year-old Varina Howell in 1845. That same year he was elected to Congress. The Mexican War began before he completed his first term. Elected colonel by a regiment of Mississippi volunteers, Davis led his troops to Mexico. After being wounded in the foot by a bullet in 1847, the governor of Mississippi appointed him to finish out the term of a U.S. senator who had died. He served in the Senate until 1850.

President Pierce appointed Davis as Secretary of War in 1853. Davis increased the size of the army, ordered improvements in uniforms and equipment, and introduced the military use of camels in the deserts of the West.

Davis returned to the Senate in 1857 but resigned on January 21, 1861, after seven Southern states seceded from the Union. Davis was unanimously elected as President of the Confederate States of America by Southern leaders in Montgomery, Alabama. His first official act was to send a peace commission to Washington in an attempt to avoid armed conflict.

When General Robert E. Lee surrendered at the end of the Civil War, Davis fled to Georgia where he was captured by Union troops. He spent nearly two years in prison because he refused to take an oath of allegiance to the United States. He was finally released after several Northerners raised the $100,000 needed for bail. Davis lived in Canada and Europe for a time. He died in New Orleans on December 6, 1889, at the age of 81.

Use what you learned about Jefferson Davis to complete the activity on page 24.

Meet Abraham Lincoln

Born in a log cabin in Kentucky in 1809, Abe Lincoln grew up in Indiana. His mother, Nancy Hanks, died when he was nine years old. A year later, his father married a widow with three children. Although he had less than a year of formal education, Lincoln learned to read and write as a young child. His stepmother, Sarah Johnston Lincoln, encouraged him to continue learning on his own.

In 1830, the Lincolns moved to Illinois where Abe split poles for fences and worked as a store clerk, surveyor, and postmaster. After studying law on his own, Lincoln became a licensed attorney in 1836. He became a well-known figure in Illinois as he traveled from city to city, often with important papers shoved inside his battered stovepipe hat.

Lincoln was defeated in his first attempt to run for public office in 1832, partly because he stopped campaigning to enlist in a volunteer army to put down a Native American rebellion.

His next attempt was successful. Lincoln was elected to the Illinois House of Representatives in 1834, 1836, 1838, and 1840.

Lincoln married Mary Todd in 1842. They had four sons, but only the oldest, Robert Todd Lincoln, lived to adulthood.

Lincoln won the election for U.S. Representative from Illinois in 1846. On many occasions, Lincoln clearly stated his belief that slavery was wrong. During the debate about whether Kansas should be a free state or a slave state, Lincoln said: "It is said that the slaveholder has the same political right to take his Negroes to Kansas that a freeman has to take his hogs or his horses. This would be true if Negroes were property in the same sense that hogs and horses are. But is this the case? It is notoriously not so."

When Lincoln ran against Stephen Douglas in 1858 for the U.S. Senate seat from Illinois, he lost by a narrow margin, but in the presidential election of 1860, he won over Douglas and two other candidates.

By the time Lincoln took office as the sixteenth president on March 4, 1861, seven Southern states had seceded from the Union. A month later, the Civil War began.

Lincoln was reelected in 1864 and lived to see the end of the Civil War on April 9, 1865. However, on April 14, 1865, Lincoln was shot while attending a play at Ford's Theatre in Washington, D.C., with his wife and another couple. He died the following day.

Use what you learned about Abraham Lincoln to complete the activity on page 24.

Name: _____ Date: _____

Compare the Leaders

Compare and contrast Jefferson Davis and Abraham Lincoln. List at least three ways the two men were similar and three ways they were different. Use the information about these two men on pages 22 and 23. Feel free to use additional reference sources for more information.

Examples: How were Jefferson Davis and Abraham Lincoln alike? Both were presidents of a country.

How were they different? Jefferson Davis had the opportunity for a more formal education.

Abraham Lincoln

Jefferson Davis

1. How Jefferson Davis and Abraham Lincoln were alike:

    _____

    _____

    _____

    _____

    _____

2. How Jefferson Davis and Abraham Lincoln were different:

    _____

    _____

    _____

    _____

    _____

Name: _____   Date: _____

The Confederate Flag

When the Civil War began, the first official Confederate flag was called the "Stars and Bars." Many people thought it looked too similar to the "Stars and Stripes," the official United States flag.

1. Color the Stars and Bars:
    Stripes: top and bottom–red; middle–white
    Rectangle: dark blue
    Stars: white

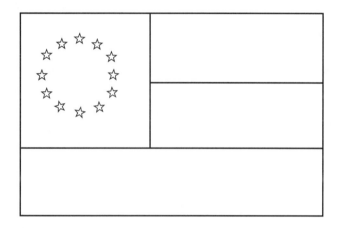

2. On May 1, 1863, this flag became the official flag of the Confederacy. Color the Confederate flag. Use reference sources to learn which colors to use.

Although there were only 11 states in the Confederacy, there were 13 stars. They represented the 11 Confederate states, plus Kentucky and Missouri. Although the Confederates expected these two states to join them, they remained loyal to the Union.

Name: _____ Date: _____

Who Started the Civil War?

The South:

- Fired the first shots at Fort Sumter.
- Seceded from the Union.
- Refused to abolish slavery.
- Insisted on states' rights over the federal government.
- Attempted to make slavery legal in new states.

The North:

- Refused to let the Southern states form their own country.
- Tried to force the South to abolish slavery.
- Put economic pressure on the South.
- Tried to prevent slavery from spreading to new states.
- Helped slaves escape, even though it was illegal.

Conditions causing the Civil War began long before the first shots were fired at Fort Sumter or when Abraham Lincoln was elected president and South Carolina decided to leave the Union.

Many compromises had been tried to iron out differences between the North and South from the time the U.S. Constitution was first written. Some worked for a while, but in the end, they all failed.

While in Congress, Lincoln proposed an emancipation program to free all slaves born after January 1, 1850, and enroll them in an apprenticeship program. He proposed that emancipation of current slaves would be voluntary, and anyone who freed his slaves would be compensated by the government.

His proposal and others for eliminating slavery gradually to avoid extreme economic hardship on Southern slaveholders were not acceptable.

Look at history from today's point of view. On your own paper, answer the following questions.

1. What is one suggestion that might have helped prevent the Civil War? Explain your idea and how it might have helped.

2. What would Northerners have liked about your idea?

3. What would Southerners have liked about your idea?

Name: _____ Date: _____

The War Begins

Shortly after the Confederate States of America formed their new government, they ordered federal troops to leave all government forts and buildings in Confederate territory.

Lincoln refused to comply with this order and pledged to maintain control of all federal property.

Major Robert Anderson commanded Fort Sumter on an island off the coast of South Carolina. When the Confederates demanded that he and his small group of men surrender the fort, he refused. On April 12, 1861, Confederate troops fired on Fort Sumter. Two days later, Major Anderson surrendered.

President Lincoln immediately called for 75,000 volunteers to join the Union Army for three months—he expected the war to be over quickly. He also declared a naval blockade of all Southern ports.

The South had few industries or natural resources. Their major crops were tobacco and cotton, cash crops they exported to Europe in exchange for food and manufactured goods. Few food crops were grown in the South.

Although about 8,000 ships were able to break through the blockade during the four years of the war, that was far less than the 20,000 that had taken goods from the South for sale to Europe and brought supplies back during the four years before the war.

1. Why do you think the Confederate government wanted all federal troops to leave the South?

   _____

   _____

2. Why do you think Lincoln refused? _____

   _____

3. Use a dictionary. What is a blockade? _____

   _____

4. How do you think a naval blockade would affect the South? _____

   _____

   _____

5. How do you think the blockade affected the South's ability to win the war?

   _____

   _____

Name: _____ Date: _____

War Is Not a Picnic

The First Battle of Bull Run was the first time that steam locomotives were used to transport troops into combat.

After the Southern victory at Fort Sumter, the next major battle of the Civil War took place at Bull Run, 35 miles south of Washington, D.C. This may have been one of the strangest battles ever fought in any war.

Hundreds of curious men, women, and children followed the Union soldiers to the battlefield on July 21, 1861. They thought it would be exciting to see a battle. They expected the war to be over quickly and wanted to see some action. When they found a good place to watch, they spread blankets and opened their picnic lunches and champagne.

As the Confederate troops headed towards Bull Run, Southern women threw flowers to their soldiers. Some set up stands to serve them lemonade. Soldiers smiled and laughed as they marched.

Suddenly, shots were fired. The battle had begun. The picnic was over. Guns and cannons roared. Soldiers were wounded and killed. At first, it seemed that the Union troops would win, but when Confederate reinforcements arrived, the Union soldiers panicked and began a disorderly retreat.

When the sightseers realized what was happening, they ran too. The onlookers found themselves in the midst of chaos as soldiers and civilians crowded the road back to Washington. Wounded men, army wagons, and ambulances surrounded the fancy coaches and buggies.

It took two days for all the Union soldiers to straggle back to the capital. The people of the city were terrified. If the Confederate Army had continued to pursue the Union troops, they may have been able to capture Washington, D.C., easily. Instead, they returned to the South and celebrated their victory.

1. Why do you think the people were so foolish to treat the battle as entertainment?

   _____

   _____

   _____

2. List ten adjectives to describe what it must have been like on the road back to Washington.

   _____

   _____

3. If the Confederate troops had captured Washington, D.C., early in the war, what advantages do you think they could have gained? Use your own paper for your answer.

Grant or Lee?

Robert E. Lee and Ulysses S. Grant were famous generals during the Civil War. One led the Union Army. The other led the Confederate Army. One accepted the surrender of the other at Appomattox Court House, Virginia.

Use reference sources to find the answers. Write "Lee" or "Grant" on the line before each statement.

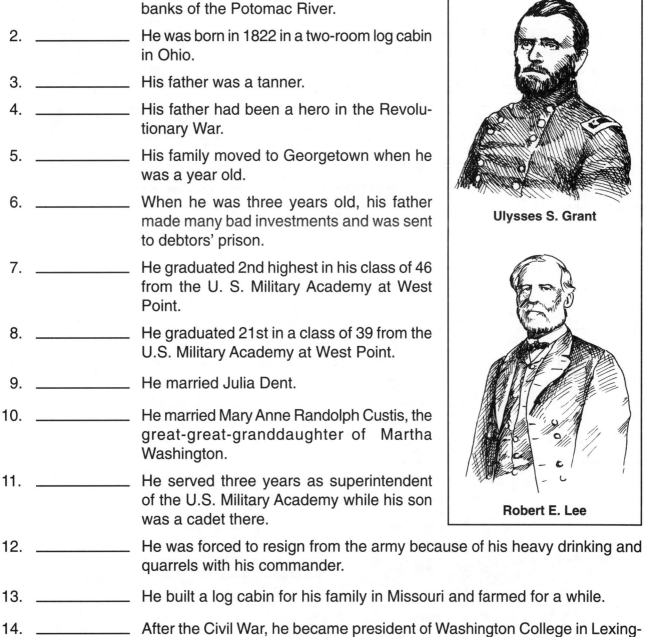

1. _____ He was born in 1807 on a plantation on the banks of the Potomac River.

2. _____ He was born in 1822 in a two-room log cabin in Ohio.

3. _____ His father was a tanner.

4. _____ His father had been a hero in the Revolutionary War.

5. _____ His family moved to Georgetown when he was a year old.

6. _____ When he was three years old, his father made many bad investments and was sent to debtors' prison.

7. _____ He graduated 2nd highest in his class of 46 from the U. S. Military Academy at West Point.

8. _____ He graduated 21st in a class of 39 from the U.S. Military Academy at West Point.

9. _____ He married Julia Dent.

10. _____ He married Mary Anne Randolph Custis, the great-great-granddaughter of Martha Washington.

11. _____ He served three years as superintendent of the U.S. Military Academy while his son was a cadet there.

Ulysses S. Grant

Robert E. Lee

12. _____ He was forced to resign from the army because of his heavy drinking and quarrels with his commander.

13. _____ He built a log cabin for his family in Missouri and farmed for a while.

14. _____ After the Civil War, he became president of Washington College in Lexington, Virginia.

15. _____ After the Civil War, he served two terms as President of the United States.

Name: _____   Date: _____

Unpopular Decisions: Income Tax and the Draft

At first, all soldiers in both the Union and Confederate Armies were volunteers. However, as the war dragged on, many died. Those who had volunteered early in the war wanted to return home.

The Federal Militia Act of 1862 gave President Lincoln authority to draft 300,000 men, but extreme opposition and additional volunteers made it unnecessary. The Confederate states also passed a Conscription Act in 1862, drafting men between the ages of 18 and 35. Because of all the exceptions and substitutions allowed, many never served in the army.

In March 1863, the federal government passed another Draft Act that applied to all men between the ages of 20 and 35 and to unmarried men between 35 and 45. The law allowed men to avoid the draft by paying a $300 fee or by hiring a substitute. Poor people felt it was unfair. Protestors rioted in working-class sections of New York City.

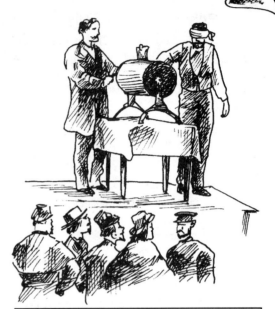

A blindfolded man pulls draft numbers at a conscription station. At first relying on volunteers, both sides eventually had to pass draft laws.

On your own paper, answer the following questions.

1. Do you think a government has the right to draft people into the army during a war? Why or why not?

2. What is your opinion of being able to avoid the draft by paying a fee or hiring a substitute?

The U.S. Congress established the Bureau of Internal Revenue on July 1, 1862. President Lincoln signed a bill making it legal for the government to collect income taxes as a temporary way to raise money for the Civil War. The income tax law was repealed in 1872.

Taxes were 3% on annual incomes between $600 and $10,000 and 5% on incomes over $10,000. Calculate the amount of taxes that would have been owed for each income listed.

Income	Taxes due
3. $ 7,028	_____
4. $10,246	_____
5. $ 3,915	_____
6. $ 599	_____
7. $ 1,040	_____
8. $14,628	_____

The Glories of War

Being a soldier during the Civil War must have been a wonderful experience, right? Not necessarily. First and foremost, thousands of soldiers died. At the Battle of Bull Run, 5,000 soldiers died. During the Battle of Spotsylvania, 12,000 men were killed in one day. By the time the war was over, 560,000 Americans were dead.

Those who lived through battles saw acre after acre of mutilated bodies. Friends and family members died. Streams and creeks ran red with blood. At times there were too many dead to bury them all.

Thousands of soldiers were wounded. Conditions in army hospitals were terrible. There were few doctors and nurses, no antibiotics, and no anesthetics. Many wounds became infected. If an arm or leg needed to be amputated, several people held the patient while the surgeon cut the limb off with a saw. Those who were lucky passed out from the pain. Even those who weren't wounded might contract a disease that could be fatal, such as typhoid. For every man in the Confederate Army who died in battle, three died from disease. Conditions in the Union Army were almost as bad.

Sometimes food was scarce, or what was available was moldy or full of bugs. Soldiers walked so many miles they wore their boots out. Then they simply wrapped rags around their feet and kept going.

Men were often scared and homesick. They missed parents, children, and wives or sweethearts. Conditions in the camps were filthy.

In winter, wood wasn't always available to use for cooking and for keeping warm. Tents offered little shelter from snow and wind. Bathrooms were open trenches dug in the ground.

In summer, heat took its toll on men marching for long distances, especially when drinking water was scarce. Keeping clean was nearly impossible most of the time. Lice and bedbugs plagued the soldiers. Rain might bring relief from the heat, but it also meant walking and sleeping in mud.

When you see photos of men happily marching off to war, remember that being a soldier in the Civil War wasn't really such a wonderful experience after all. In spite of that, many brave soldiers did what they considered their duty: to fight for the cause they thought was right.

Name: _____ Date: _____

Letters From a Soldier

Use the information from the previous page and reference sources to learn more about what it was like to be a soldier during the Civil War.

Imagine being a fifteen-year-old soldier in the Civil War. Write four short letters he might have written to his parents. Use your own paper if you need more room.

Letter #1: Describe your first few days as a soldier. _____

_____

_____

_____

_____

Letter #2: Describe conditions in your camp and how you and the other soldiers feel after marching over 100 miles in a week.

_____

_____

_____

_____

_____

Letter #3: Describe how you feel the night before your first battle. _____

_____

_____

_____

_____

Letter #4: Describe how you feel after your first battle: your side lost, and several of your friends were killed.

_____

_____

_____

_____

_____

Name: _____ Date: _____

Quilt It

During the 1800s, women made quilts by hand-sewing pieces of fabric together to form a pattern. The fabric was cut from different pieces of old or outgrown clothing. They attached a backing and stuffed the middle with a soft material such as cotton, goose down, or wool. To keep the stuffing in place, they sewed through all three layers, usually in a decorative pattern.

Since women had few outlets for artistic expression or for voicing their opinions about politics, quilts became a way to create something beautiful and expressive.

Besides being beautiful, quilts had a very practical purpose: they helped keep people warm on cold winter nights. Abolitionist groups sold quilts to raise funds to help fugitive slaves.

Women sometimes worked together by making individual squares, then sewing the squares together to finish the quilt. This helped them finish their quilts more quickly and gave them an opportunity to visit with their friends and discuss the current issues while they worked.

Select one of the following quilting projects.

1. Hold a quilting bee.

    Each person in the group makes one or more paper quilt squares. Each person creates a design to represent a person, place, or event from the Civil War.

    For each quilt square, cut graph paper or construction paper into an eight-inch square. Draw and color or cut and glue paper to complete your design on the graph paper. Suggestions: wallpaper scraps, color ads from magazines, wrapping paper, etc.

    When finished, join quilt squares together with tape on the back side. Display the finished quilt for everyone to enjoy.

2. Make your own quilt.

    Create two to four designs in color that represent people, places, or events from the Civil War. Use eight-inch squares of paper.

    Photocopy your designs in color. Make enough copies to form a quilt with 4″ x 4″ or 5″ x 5″ squares. Join the squares together with tape on the back side, alternating the designs to form a pattern.

Name: _____ Date: _____

Get to Know Someone

Read a biography or autobiography of a person who lived during the Civil War. Then fill in the lines below with information from the book. A list of possible titles can be found on pages 59–60.

Title of book: _____

Author of book: _____

Person's name: _____

Date of birth: _____

Place of birth: _____

Date of death: _____

Briefly describe the main character: _____

_____

Where did this person live during the Civil War? _____

What were this person's views on slavery? _____

_____

_____

What were this person's views on secession? _____

_____

_____

Describe one interesting incident from the book. _____

_____

_____

How did the Civil War affect this person? _____

_____

_____

Would you recommend this book to others? Why or why not? _____

_____

_____

Name: _____ Date: _____

What Did They Wear?

When people think of soldiers in the Civil War, they often think of Union troops in blue and Confederate troops in gray uniforms. Sometimes that was not the case.

Both the Northern and Southern armies were made up mostly of volunteers. Some volunteer groups had their own uniforms that were completely different from the standard. The New York 79th Infantry soldiers (Union Highlanders) wore kilts to battle, while the Louisiana Tiger Zouaves (Confederate) wore a short gold jacket, wide trousers, and a red cap.

Use the key at the right to color the standard uniforms of the Union and Confederate Armies.

A. Tan	B. Gray	C. Light Blue
D. Dark Blue	E. Yellow	F. Black
G. Brown		

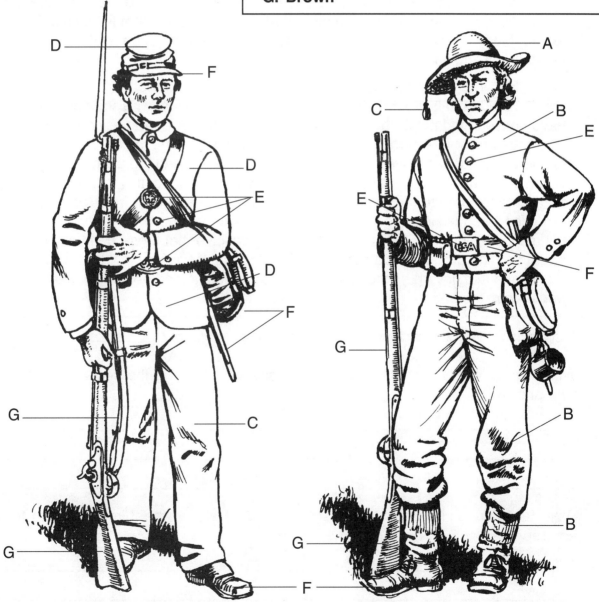

Union Standard Uniform   **Confederate Standard Uniform**

35

Name: _____ Date: _____

The Gettysburg Address

President Lincoln delivered his famous speech, the Gettysburg Address, on November 19, 1863, at a ceremony dedicating the cemetery to soldiers who had died in the Battle of Gettysburg. Over 50,000 Union and Confederate soldiers died or were wounded in the battle.

Lincoln's Gettysburg Address

Fourscore and seven years ago our fathers brought forth on this continent a new nation, conceived in liberty and dedicated to the proposition that all men are created equal.

Now we are engaged in a great civil war, testing whether that nation or any nation so conceived and so dedicated can long endure. We are met on a great battlefield of that war. We have come to dedicate a portion of that field, as a final resting-place for those who here gave their lives that that nation might live. It is altogether fitting and proper that we should do this.

But, in a larger sense, we can not dedicate—we can not consecrate—we can not hallow—this ground. The brave men, living and dead, who struggled here, have consecrated it, far above our poor power to add or detract. The world will little note, nor long remember, what we say here, but it can never forget what they did here. It is for us the living, rather, to be dedicated here to the unfinished work which they who fought here have thus far so nobly advanced. It is rather for us to be here dedicated to the great task remaining before us—that from these honored dead we take increased devotion to that cause for which they gave the last full measure of devotion—that we here highly resolve that these dead shall not have died in vain—that this nation, under God, shall have a new birth of freedom—and that government of the people, by the people, for the people, shall not perish from the earth.

---

1. A score is 20 years. How long is fourscore and seven years? _____

2. What was Lincoln's purpose for giving this speech? Refer to the second paragraph for your answer.

  _____

  _____

  _____

3. What tasks does Lincoln say must still be done? Refer to the third paragraph for your answer.

  _____

  _____

  _____

Name: _____ Date: _____

Create a Civil War Memorial

Memorials honoring people, places, and events have been made in many shapes and sizes and from many different types of materials. Paintings, songs, quilts, buildings, museums, parks, and statues are types of memorials.

The Lincoln Memorial in Washington, D.C., is a magnificent building of marble, granite, and limestone honoring Abraham Lincoln.

In Georgia, Jefferson Davis Memorial Park marks the site where Davis was captured by Union troops in 1865.

The Vietnam Veterans Memorial, a V-shaped black granite wall, was engraved with the names of over 58,000 men and women who died in that war.

The faces of George Washington, Thomas Jefferson, Theodore Roosevelt, and Abraham Lincoln were carved into the granite wall of Mount Rushmore as a memorial to those four presidents.

1. Design a memorial honoring any person, place, or event from the Civil War. On your own paper, use words and illustrations to describe how the memorial would look and why you selected that person, place, or event. Include information about the memorial's location, size, shape, color, and materials used. Use the lines below for notes.

_____

_____

_____

_____

_____

_____

_____

_____

_____

_____

Name: _____ Date: _____

Hundreds of Battles Fought

    The Civil War was a costly and lengthy one for both the Union and the Confederacy. Beginning with the battle at Fort Sumter on April 12, 1861, the war continued until General Robert E. Lee surrendered at Appomattox Court House on April 9, 1865.

    Both sides achieved many victories and suffered many defeats. Battles were fought on land and at sea; as far north as Gettysburg, Pennsylvania, and as far south as Florida and New Orleans.

Use reference sources to learn more about one Civil War battle. On your own paper, write a newspaper article about the battle. In your article, answer these questions:

- Who commanded the Union Army in that battle?
- Who commanded the Confederate Army in that battle?
- When and where was this battle fought? Who won?
- Why was this battle fought, and why was it important?
- What did both sides hope to accomplish?
- How did this battle affect the outcome of the Civil War?

Some battles fought during the Civil War were:

Antietam	Gettysburg
Atlanta	Holly Springs
Baton Rouge	Huntsville
Bent Creek	Kennesaw Mountain
Brandy Station	Mechanicsville
Bull Run	Milliken's Bend
Chancellorsville	Missionary Ridge
Chattanooga	Murfreesboro
Chickamauga	Nashville
Chickasaw Bluffs	New Orleans
Cold Harbor	Pea Ridge
Corinth	Shiloh
Fort Donelson	Spotsylvania
Fort Henry	Vicksburg
Fort Sumter	The Wilderness
Fredericksburg	

Name: _____ Date: _____

The First Air Corps

In 1861, 42 years before the Wright brothers made their first airplane flight, President Lincoln named Thaddeus Lowe Chief Aeronaut of the Army of the Potomac.

What was an aeronaut? At that time, it was a person who flew a hot air balloon.

Lowe recruited and managed the North's first hot air balloon corps, which provided aerial surveillance during the first two years of the Civil War. He and his airship crew made over 3,000 flights into Confederate territory.

Confederate General James Longstreet remarked, "The Federals had been using balloons in examining our positions, and we watched with envious eyes their beautiful observation as they floated high in the air, well out of range of our guns."

The first Confederate balloons were made of varnished cotton and inflated with air heated by burning pine knots and turpentine. These were tethered to half-mile ropes connected to a windlass. Cotton was not a satisfactory material for hot air balloons, but the cost of silk, the best material, was too expensive. The Confederates overcame this problem by sewing together pieces of silk from dresses donated by Southern women to make a balloon.

At the Battle of Fair Oaks in May 1862, Lowe's observations from a hydrogen balloon provided vital information, which narrowly averted a Union defeat, according to his unpublished memoirs. Despite the advantage of air surveillance, many Union generals were not convinced of its value, and the air corps was expensive to maintain. When Lowe quit in 1863, the air corps itself was discontinued.

On August 3, 1861, the U.S.S. *Fanny* became the country's first aircraft carrier. Aeronaut John LaMountain used the ship as a base for a balloon survey of Southern activity along the Potomac River. From the air, an observer could get a much fuller picture of the scene below, including numbers and placement of troops.

1. Use a dictionary. Define *aerial*. _____

   _____

2. Use a dictionary. Define *surveillance*. _____

   _____

3. How do you think the use of hot air balloons gave the North an advantage?

   _____

   _____

   _____

   _____

Name: _____	Date: _____

The War at Sea

Except for a few gunboats at the beginning of the Civil War, the South had no ships to protect its 3,500-mile coastline from Virginia to Texas. Union ships patrolled the Atlantic coast and the Gulf of Mexico, blocking Confederate trade routes. This prevented the South from receiving supplies or sending cotton, tobacco, and other trade goods to be sold.

Stephen Mallory, Confederate Secretary of the Navy, decided the South needed an iron-clad ship. They raised the U.S.S. *Merrimac,* which had been sunk at the beginning of the war to prevent it from falling into Confederate hands. They covered the ship with iron plating and renamed it the C.S.S. *Virginia.*

When the North learned about the C.S.S. *Virginia*, they decided to build their own iron-clad ship, the U.S.S. *Monitor*. By then, the South had a three-month head start.

Both navies rushed to complete their ships. Many people expected the ironclads to sink as soon as they were launched. They didn't sink, but both had serious problems, and there was no time to fix everything.

In its first battle at Hampton Roads on March 8, 1862, the *Virginia* destroyed two Union warships, caused one to become grounded, and drove off two others.

The *Monitor* arrived the following day, before the *Virginia* could destroy the ship that had run aground. Only 50 yards apart at times, the two ironclads blasted cannonballs at each other. The crews of both fought desperately to keep their ships afloat. When cannonballs failed to sink the *Monitor*, the *Virginia* tried to ram the ship, but missed by only a few feet. After a four-hour battle, the *Monitor* headed for water too shallow for the *Virginia* to follow.

When the *Virginia* arrived at Gosport, they discovered the ship had been hit by cannonballs at least 150 times. After being repaired, the *Virginia* returned to Hampton Roads on April 11, where the *Monitor* and a pack of Union warships waited. Outnumbered and surrounded, the crew set the *Virginia* on fire. It burned until it finally exploded. The *Monitor* later sank in a December storm.

The South built 22 ironclad ships, but the North built more than 60. With their superior numbers, the Union tightened the blockade, captured most of the major ports in the South, and controlled inland rivers.

Use what you've learned about the ironclads to write a test for a partner on your own paper. Write 10 questions; they can be true and false, matching, or fill in the blanks. Trade papers with a partner, and take each other's tests.

40

Name: _____ Date: _____

The Story Behind the Song

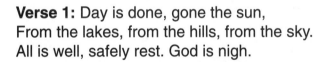

The haunting melody of "Taps" often brings tears to the eyes of listeners. The story behind the song is a sad one too.

In 1862, Union Army Captain Robert Ellicombe and his men were fighting near Harrison's Landing, Virginia. The Confederate Army was on the other side of a narrow strip of land. During the night, Captain Ellicombe heard the moans of a wounded soldier.

He risked his life to bring the wounded man back for medical attention. When he finally dragged the soldier back to the Union lines, he discovered the man, a Confederate soldier, had died. Not only that, the soldier was Captain Ellicombe's son who had been studying music in the South when the Civil War began.

The next morning, the grief-stricken father asked permission to give his son a full military burial, even though he was an enemy soldier. He also requested that Army band members play at the funeral. His superiors would not allow the band to play.

However, they did allow him to select one musician. Captain Ellicombe asked a bugler to play the music he had found on a piece of paper in his son's pocket. That music was the song "Taps." Here are the words to this song.

Verse 1: Day is done, gone the sun,
From the lakes, from the hills, from the sky.
All is well, safely rest. God is nigh.

Verse 2: Fading light, dims the sight,
And a star gems the sky, gleaming bright.
From afar, drawing nigh, falls the night.

Verse 3: Thanks and praise, for our days,
'Neath the sun, 'neath the stars, 'neath the sky,
As we go, this we know, God is nigh.

Many other songs that were written or became popular during the Civil War are still played today. Select one of the songs listed, or another Civil War song found on the Internet or from other references sources. On another sheet of paper, write the words to two verses. Add information about when or why the song was written and what you think the words mean.

Confederate Songs
The Bonnie Blue Flag
Dixie
The Yellow Rose of Texas
Stonewall Jackson's Way
Tramp! Tramp! Tramp!
Maryland, My Maryland
Goober Peas

Union songs
Battle Hymn of the Republic
Marching Through Georgia
John Brown's Body
Marching Along
Tramp! Tramp! Tramp!
The Battle Cry of Freedom
Give Us a Flag

Name: _____ Date: _____

What Did They Eat?

These foods were commonly eaten during the Civil War period. Write the words from the word bank on the lines to match the definitions. Use a dictionary or other reference sources.

buttermilk	chitlins	cobbler	collard greens
cracklings	dodgers	fatback	grits
hardtack	hog jowls	hog maws	Hoppin' John
hush puppies	Johnnycakes	okra	salt pork

A. _____ Cereal made from coarsely ground corn

B. _____ Fat from the back of a pig used to make lard or cracklings

C. _____ Made from small intestines of pigs

D. _____ Pigskin fried until crispy brown

E. _____ Liquid left over after milk was churned

F. _____ Deep-fried cornmeal dumplings

G. _____ Pancakes made with cornmeal

H. _____ Cornmeal cakes baked until very hard

I. _____ Black-eyed peas cooked with salt pork and seasoning, traditionally served on New Year's Day for good luck

J. _____ A plant grown in the South used to thicken soups and stews

K. _____ Cheeks of a hog cut into squares and cured or smoked

L. _____ A cracker-like biscuit made of flour, water, and salt, commonly eaten by soldiers during the Civil War

M. _____ Salt-cured pork from the pig's belly or sides

N. _____ The tops of a plant similar to kale; leaves can be cooked and eaten

O. _____ A fruit-filled dessert

P. _____ Pig stomach

Name: _____ Date: _____

Women and the Civil War

All the leaders in both the North and South during the Civil War were White men. Women were not allowed to vote. They had no say in politics. They were not allowed to join the army. Men thought women should stay at home and take care of their children and homes.

But that doesn't mean women weren't affected by the war or that they did not participate. When the men joined the army, the women were left to run the homes, businesses, farms, and plantations. They planted and plowed fields and harvested crops. They did their best to keep their families together until the men returned. Sadly, many men never returned.

When male teachers joined the army, women kept the schools running. When there was a shortage of male factory workers in the North, women also learned to fill those jobs.

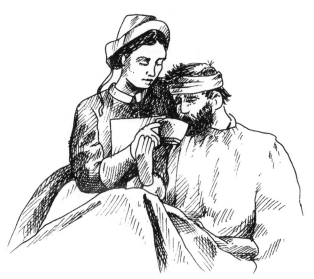

Women helped tend the large number of injured and sick soldiers, kept the hospitals as clean as possible, and ran convalescent homes. Clara Barton, founder of the American Red Cross, and Louisa May Alcott, a famous writer, worked as nurses during the Civil War. Dorothea Dix, known for her reform work in prisons and hospitals, was put in charge of recruiting and training nurses.

Women raised money through bake sales and carnivals to buy supplies for troops. They knitted socks and made clothing for the soldiers.

Some women became spies. Pauline Cushman, an actress, traveled to the South and returned with information for the Union Army. Harriet Tubman, an escaped slave, served the Union Army as a cook, spy, nurse, and scout, but she was never paid for her work.

During the four long years of the Civil War, women learned new skills and found they could be self-reliant. They were able to do many of the same jobs as men. Yet when the men returned from the war, they expected women to quietly accept their former subservient roles. More and more women came to believe they were entitled to equal rights.

1. How would you have felt if you had been a woman who had worked a full-time job plus taken care of a home and children for several years during the war, and then was expected to return to your former role after the war?

_____

_____

_____

_____

_____

Name: _____ Date: _____

What If?

What if the North and South had not fought the Civil War and had remained two separate countries? Keep in mind how Southerners felt about states' rights as opposed to a strong central government.

1. How do you think history would be different?_____

_____

_____

_____

2. How do you think your life today would be different?_____

_____

_____

_____

3. What if the South had won the Civil War? _____

_____

_____

_____

4. How do you think history would be different? _____

_____

_____

5. How do you think your life today would be different?_____

_____

_____

6. What if slavery were still legal in the United States?_____

_____

_____

7. On your own paper, write a "What if?" question about the Civil War and answer it.

Name: _____ Date: _____

The Emancipation Proclamation

On January 1, 1863, President Lincoln issued the Emancipation Proclamation, which freed slaves in all states or parts of states that were in rebellion against the United States.

The Emancipation Proclamation actually freed only about one million slaves. It didn't apply to the three million slaves in states that had not seceded from the Union or even in certain areas of states that had seceded. The states that had formed the Confederacy ignored the order. Slaves remained slaves.

In the Emancipation Proclamation, Lincoln declared that the government, army, and navy would recognize and maintain the freedom of slaves and would do nothing to stop them from any efforts "they may make for their actual freedom."

Lincoln knew that most slave owners would not willingly free their slaves. He did not want to encourage slaves to revolt or to use violence if it could be avoided. In the words of Lincoln:

"... I hereby enjoin upon the people so declared to be free to abstain from all violence, unless in necessary self-defence; and I recommend to them that, in all cases when allowed, they labor faithfully for reasonable wages."

It wasn't until after the Civil War ended and the Thirteenth Amendment passed in 1865, that slavery was officially abolished everywhere in the United States. Even then, slaves were not considered "citizens," and even male slaves did not have the right to vote.

On your own paper, answer the following questions:

1. How do you think slaves felt when they learned about the Emancipation Proclamation?

2. How do you think slaves in places not covered by the Emancipation Proclamation felt when they learned the news?

3. What do you think Lincoln meant when he said the above words? Rewrite what Lincoln said in your own words.

4. Since there were no radios or TVs, and few slaves could read, how do you think slaves learned about the Emancipation Proclamation?

Name: _____ Date: _____

Black Soldiers Help Win the War

Black soldiers had fought in the Revolutionary War and in the War of 1812, but when they first volunteered to fight in the Civil War, they were refused. Although abolitionists urged President Lincoln to accept Blacks as soldiers, the majority of politicians opposed the idea, believing that Blacks could not learn the duties and become good soldiers.

Frederick Douglass, an escaped slave, questioned this decision. "Why does the government reject the Negro? Is he not a man? Can he not wield a sword, fire a gun, march and countermarch, and obey orders like any other?"

Finally, after two years of war, Congress passed the Militia Act of 1862 allowing the president to employ Blacks "for any military or naval service for which they may be found competent."

The first Black Union regiment, the 54th Massachusetts Volunteers, received only $10 a month as salary, $3 less than White soldiers. Blacks were not permitted to hold a rank higher than captain.

Union regiments of Black soldiers in South Carolina consisted mostly of former slaves, men who knew the territory and had strong motives to fight against their former masters for the freedom of their fellow slaves.

At first, Blacks were assigned only to menial tasks like cleaning latrines and building roads. Before the war ended, however, more than 186,000 Blacks fought in the Union Army and participated in over 400 battles.

Although some White soldiers welcomed the addition of Black troops, many objected strongly. Some officers refused to lead Black soldiers. Some White soldiers refused to fight beside Blacks. In spite of their bravery and outstanding records, discrimination against Black soldiers continued for nearly another 100 years. It wasn't until 1948 that the army ended segregation, and Black and White soldiers worked side by side.

Faced with a critical shortage of manpower, Jefferson Davis signed the Negro Soldier Law on March 13, 1865. Units of Black soldiers were organized in Richmond. Southern crowds threw mud and stones at the soldiers as they trained. However, the war ended soon after, and the Confederate Black soldiers never fought in the Civil War.

1. Why do you think Blacks would have been willing to join the Confederate Army?

_____

_____

_____

_____

_____

Name: _____ Date: _____

Fact or Opinion?

A **fact** is a statement that can be verified as true.

Fact: The Civil War began in 1861.

An **opinion** is a statement that cannot be verified as true.

Opinion: The Southern states were right to secede.

Write "F" for fact or "O" for opinion on the line by each statement.

1. _____ Abraham Lincoln was the best president.

2. _____ Abraham Lincoln was the sixteenth U.S. President.

3. _____ Slavery was legal in the United States.

4. _____ Slaves did not deserve any rights.

5. _____ Robert E. Lee was a great general.

6. _____ Many Northerners did not want Blacks to have equal rights.

7. _____ Thousands of people read *Uncle Tom's Cabin* because it was such a great book.

8. _____ Abolitionists were right to help slaves escape even if it meant breaking the law.

9. _____ People who lived in the new territories had the right to decide for themselves if they wanted to allow slavery or not.

10. _____ Lincoln lost the campaign for U.S. Senate in 1858.

11. Write two facts about the Civil War.

   _____

   _____

   _____

12. Write two opinions about the Civil War.

   _____

   _____

   _____

Name: _____ Date: _____

Interview a Union Soldier

You are a reporter for a Southern newspaper in 1863. Your boss sent you to interview a Union soldier and write an article about the Civil War from the Union point of view.

What is the name, age, and former occupation of the person you will interview?

_____

Write 12 questions you might ask that person during an interview.

1. _____

2. _____

3. _____

4. _____

5. _____

6. _____

7. _____

8. _____

9. _____

10. _____

11. _____

12. _____

Name: _____ Date: _____

North or South?

There were many differences between the North and the South during the Civil War. Use reference sources if you need help. Write "N" for North or "S" for South on the line before each phrase. Write "N/S" if the phrase applies to both.

1. _____ Population about 9 million

2. _____ Population about 20 million

3. _____ Mainly agricultural

4. _____ Women could not vote

5. _____ No power mills

6. _____ Highly industrial

7. _____ No formal army

8. _____ No formal navy

9. _____ Wore homespun uniforms because they had no factories to make cloth

10. _____ Many shipyards

11. _____ Produced about 97 percent of the nation's firearms

12. _____ Had more coal, iron, and copper

13. _____ Grew enough food not to need imported food

14. _____ Grew mainly cash crops, not food

15. _____ Tried to get England and France to join them

16. _____ Wanted to keep England and France out of the war

17. Of the items listed, which do you think most helped the Union Army win the Civil War? Why?

    _____

    _____

18. Of the items listed, which do you think most caused the South to lose the Civil War? Why?

    _____

    _____

Name: _____   Date: _____

Then and Now

Read the statements about conditions in the past. Add a statement about conditions today.

Then: People walked, rode horses, or stagecoaches to travel. Even a 20-mile journey could be long and difficult.

Now: _____

_____

Then: The North and South disagreed strongly on many issues, especially states' rights and slavery.

Now: _____

_____

Then: Prisoners of war became slaves. Some people were forced into slavery as a form of punishment because they could not pay their debts.

Now: _____

_____

Then: Even in the North where slavery was illegal, Blacks were not allowed to attend the same churches and schools as Whites.

Now: _____

_____

Then: People in the 1860s did not have electricity or running water in their homes.

Now: _____

_____

Then: Hot air balloons were used for surveillance during the Civil War.

Now: _____

_____

Then: Abraham Lincoln was President of the United States.

Now: _____

_____

Name: _____ Date: _____

Interview a Confederate Soldier

You are a reporter for a Northern newspaper in 1863. Your boss sent you to interview a Confederate soldier and write an article about the Civil War from the Confederate point of view.

What is the name, age, and former occupation of the person you will interview?

_____

Write 12 questions you might ask that person during an interview.

1. _____
   _____

2. _____
   _____

3. _____
   _____

4. _____
   _____

5. _____
   _____

6. _____
   _____

7. _____
   _____

8. _____
   _____

9. _____
   _____

10. _____
    _____

11. _____
    _____

12. _____
    _____

Name: _____ Date: _____

Scavenger Hunt

To complete this scavenger hunt, use the Internet and other reference materials to find the answers.

1. The first battle of the Civil War took place at Fort Sumter.
   A. In what state is Fort Sumter? _____
   B. For whom was it named? _____
   C. What geometric shape was Fort Sumter? _____

2. Who was president when the first Southern state seceded from the Union?
   _____

3. What was Robert E. Lee's horse's name? _____

4. A Confederate submarine was the first to sink an enemy ship. What was the name of the submarine? _____

5. His real name was Hiram Ulysses Grant. How did it get changed to Ulysses S. Grant?
   _____
   _____

6. What did the "S" stand for in Ulysses S. Grant's name? _____

7. In 1861 the King of Siam offered to send a gift to the United States, but Lincoln politely refused. What gift did he turn down? _____

8. Who was vice president during Lincoln's first term as president? _____

9. The "Battle Hymn of the Republic," was written in 1861, shortly after the Civil War began. Who wrote it? _____

10. Who was the Confederate general who gave the order to open fire on Fort Sumter on April 12, 1861? _____

11. Nicknamed "Moses," she led more than 300 slaves to freedom. During the Civil War, she served the Union Army as a cook, spy, nurse, and scout, but she was never paid for her work. She later opened a home for the aged in New York. Who was she?
    _____

12. What was the name of the man who attempted to end slavery through force by leading a raid on the arsenal at Harpers Ferry in October 1859?
    _____

Name: _____ Date: _____

Surrender at Appomattox Court House

After four long years of war, the armies of both the Union and the Confederacy had lost thousands of men. During a ten-month siege of Richmond, Virginia, the capital of the Confederacy, supplies for the Confederate troops became scarce. Many were ill. Thousands deserted. Finally on the night of April 2, 1865, General Lee ordered his troops to retreat west across the James River. Union troops took Richmond and continued a running battle with the rear guard of the retreating troops.

General Lee and his disheartened troops expected to find food waiting at the village of Amelia Courthouse. There they found military supplies, but no food. They continued retreating.

General Grant realized that if he continued to push his advantage, there was a good chance General Lee would surrender. President Lincoln agreed and gave the order to proceed.

For six days, Lee's men continued to fight as they fled west 90 miles. When they arrived at the small village of Appomattox Court House, they again discovered supplies of food had not arrived.

Virginia Colonel Magnus Thompson described the troops: "The few men who still carried their muskets had hardly the appearance of soldiers—their clothes all tattered and covered with mud, their eyes sunken and lusterless ..."

General Grant sent a message under a flag of truce offering to accept Lee's surrender. On April 9, 1865, General Robert E. Lee sent his reply: "I received your note this morning ... with references to the surrender of this army. I now request an interview in accordance with ... that purpose."

Grant ordered an immediate cease-fire. The two generals met in the front parlor of a two-story brick farmhouse. According to the terms of the agreement, General Lee surrendered all men and officers and all arms, ammunition, and supplies except the horses and mules that were the personal property of the soldiers.

General Lee offered to return about 1,000 Union soldiers who were being held as prisoners of war because he had no food to feed them. Grant accepted his offer and then sent beef, bread, coffee, and sugar to feed the Confederate troops.

When Union soldiers began firing cannon salutes to celebrate the end of the war, General Grant ordered all loud celebrations ended. "The war is over, the rebels are our countrymen again," he told them.

On your own paper, describe how you think Lee felt when he was forced to surrender.

Name: _____ Date: _____

After the War

When the Civil War was finally over, 620,000 Americans had died. Thousands more had been wounded or were seriously ill. Men returned to their families blind, deaf, or missing arms and legs. Families lost sons, fathers, brothers, and husbands. Over one-fifth of the adult White males in the South had died. Another 37,000 African-Americans had died fighting for their freedom.

Families were split apart. Brothers had fought each other. Kentucky's Senator John Crittenden had had two sons who were generals in the Civil War: one serving in the Confederate Army, the other in the Union Army. In some families, the bitter feelings caused by the war never healed.

Property damage was so extensive in the South that some areas took years to recover. Farmland was ruined and farm animals had been killed. Cities were in ruins; homes had been burned, crops destroyed, and railroad lines torn up. Confederate money was worthless.

The slaves were free, but free to do what? Most had no land, no homes, no education, no money, and no skills.

1. Imagine being a woman with four children. Your home was burned down during the war. All your farm animals were killed. When your husband returns, he is an invalid and cannot do any kind of work. What can you do to pick up the pieces and start a new life?

    _____

    _____

    _____

    _____

    _____

    _____

2. Imagine being a former male slave in the South. You are free at last but have nowhere to go, no home, no money, and no skills other than working in a cotton field. You have a wife and two children living with you. Your other two children were sold to a different master, and you have no idea where they are. How do you feel about your freedom?

    _____

    _____

    _____

    _____

    _____

    _____

Name: _____ Date: _____

Order, Please

Number the events in order from 1 (first) to 10 (last). Use the time line at the beginning of this book for reference.

A. _____ General Lee surrendered at Appomattox Court House.

B. _____ Jefferson Davis was elected president of the Confederacy.

C. _____ Abraham Lincoln was elected president for his first term.

D. _____ The Thirteenth Amendment abolished slavery.

E. _____ South Carolina seceded from the Union.

F. _____ Lincoln delivered the Gettysburg Address.

G. _____ *Uncle Tom's Cabin* was published.

H. _____ Lincoln issued the Emancipation Proclamation.

I. _____ President Lincoln was assassinated.

J. _____ The Battle at Fort Sumter was fought.

K. Write two historical events that occurred before the Civil War.

_____

_____

_____

_____

L. Write two historical events that occurred after the Civil War.

_____

_____

_____

_____

Name: _____ Date: _____

True or False?

Circle "T" for True or "F" for False.

1.   T   F   Abraham Lincoln and Jefferson Davis were both candidates in the presidential election of 1860.

2.   T   F   The first battle of the Civil War was fought at Fort Sumter.

3.   T   F   All slaves in the United States were prisoners of war.

4.   T   F   According to the fugitive slave laws, if a slave escaped to a free state, he or she was automatically free.

5.   T   F   The majority of Southerners lived on large plantations and had hundreds of slaves.

6.   T   F   For many years, slavery was legal in all colonies, North and South.

7.   T   F   Slavery was illegal according to the U.S. Constitution when it was first written.

8.   T   F   *Uncle Tom's Cabin* was a fictional story about slavery written by Harriet Beecher Stowe.

9.   T   F   Many slaves escaped through the Underground Railroad.

10.   T   F   Abolitionists were people who tried to end slavery.

11.   T   F   General Robert E. Lee was commander in chief of the Union Army.

12.   T   F   South Carolina was the first Southern state to secede.

13.   T   F   The colors of the Confederate flag were green, orange, and black.

14.   T   F   The Gettysburg Address was a famous debate between Abraham Lincoln and Stephen Douglas.

15.   T   F   Both the North and South used hot air balloons during the Civil War.

Civil War Projects

Select one of these ideas for a project. Work alone, with a partner, or with a small group if appropriate.

- Give a ten-minute abolitionist speech to a group.

- Write about the history of your community during the years of the Civil War (1860 to 1865).

- Write the words to a song that could have been sung by soldiers from the Union or Confederate Army. Make up your own melody or use one you know.

- Make an audio or videotape of an interview with a freedman, a fugitive slave, an abolitionist, a slave owner, or a Civil War soldier.

- Dress like Abraham Lincoln and recite the Gettysburg Address from memory to the class.

- Hold a debate on one of these issues:

    Admitting Missouri as a slave state

    The Fugitive Slave Law of 1850

    The *Dred Scott* case

    The secession of South Carolina

- Draw a historically-correct illustration of a Civil War battle.

- Plan a menu for a party that includes only items available in the 1860s. Include the recipe for each item on the menu.

- Design and sew a flag that could represent the conflict in the United States during the Civil War.

- Learn about Christmas or another holiday celebrated in the 1860s. Create a display showing how the holiday was celebrated. Include illustrations of decorations, clothing, gifts, foods, activities, etc.

- Make a board game related to the Civil War. Include the board and game pieces needed and a copy of the rules. Play the game with at least three different people. Ask for their opinions of the game.

- Learn about what children in the 1860s did for fun. Give a demonstration of at least three games or other activities children enjoyed. Include illustrations and/or the actual items needed to play the game.

- Make a collage of military uniforms and items used by soldiers during the Civil War. Use pictures downloaded from the Internet, photocopied from books, or draw your own.

Report on the Civil War

Learn more about one of the people listed below who had an impact on history at the time of the American Civil War. Use the Internet and other reference sources to write a three- to five-page report. Add illustrations and maps if appropriate.

Julia Ward Howe

Dorothea Dix

Louisa May Alcott	Stonewall Jackson
Clara Barton	Joseph Johnston
Pierre Beauregard	Robert E. Lee
Belle Boyd	Abraham Lincoln
Braxton Bragg	George B. McClellan
John Brown	Wilmer McLean
Ambrose Burnside	George Meade
Benjamin Butler	William Passmore
Pauline Cushman	George Pickett
Jefferson Davis	John Pope
Dorothea Dix	Roswell Ripley
Stephen Douglas	John Scobell
Frederick Douglass	Dred Scott
Samuel Dupont	Winfield Scott
Emma Edmonds	Philip Sheridan
David Farragut	William T. Sherman
William Garrison	Robert Smalls
Ulysses S. Grant	Harriet Beecher Stowe
John Grayson	J.E.B. Stuart
Henry W. Halleck	Sojourner Truth
Charles Heidsick	Harriet Tubman
Joseph Hooker	Nat Turner
Julia Ward Howe	Elizabeth Van Lew

Clara Barton

William T. Sherman

58

Suggested Reading

Nonfiction:

North by Night: A Story of the Underground Railroad by Katherine Ayers

Harpers Ferry: The Story of John Brown's Raid by Tracy Barret

The Civil War A to Z by Norman Bolotin

The Story of Fort Sumter by Eugenia Burney

Civil War: Garments, History, Legends, and Lore by Gina Capaldi

Battle of the Ironclads: The Monitor and the Merrimack by Alden R. Carter

A Separate Battle: Women and the Civil War by Ina Chang

The Civil War: 1860–1865 by Christopher and James Collier

Slavery and the Coming of the Civil War by Christopher and James Collier

The Dred Scott Case: Slavery and Citizenship by D.J. Herda

If You Traveled on the Underground Railroad by Ellen Levine

The Story of the Battle of Bull Run by Zachary Kent

The Story of the Surrender at Appomattox Court House by Zachary Kent

The Story of Sherman's March to the Sea by Zachary Kent

Rebels Against Slavery: American Slave Revolts by Patricia MacKissack

Behind the Blue and Gray: The Soldier's Life in the Civil War by Delia Ray

Civil War Soldiers by Catherine Reef

The Gettysburg Address by Kenneth Richards

Freedom Train by Dorothy Sterling

Biographies and Autobiographies

John Brown: Antislavery Activist by Helaine Becker

Frederick Douglass Fights for Freedom by Margaret Davidson

Go Free or Die: A Story About Harriet Tubman by Jeri Ferris

Suggested Reading

Walking the Road to Freedom: A Story About Sojourner Truth by Jeri Ferris

Stonewall Jackson: Lee's Right Hand by Chris Hughes

Robert E. Lee: Leader of the Confederate Army by David King

Harriet and the Runaway Book: The Story of Harriet Beecher Stowe and <u>Uncle Tom's Cabin</u>
    by Johanna Johnston

Journey to Freedom: Frederick Douglass by John Passaro

Harriet Tubman: Conductor on the Underground Railroad by Ann Petry

Escape From Slavery: Five Journeys to Freedom by Doreen Rappaport

Harriet Tubman by John Rowley

Black Crusaders for Freedom edited by Bennet Wayne

Fiction

The Tin Heart by Karen Ackerman

Thunder at Gettysburg by Patricia Lee Gauch

Which Way Freedom? by Joyce Hansen

Three Against the Tide by D. Anne Love

Cecil's Story by George-Ella Lyon

Christmas in the Big House, Christmas in the Quarters by Patricia and Fredrick MacKissack

Pink and Say by Patricia Polacco

*Meet Addy; Addy Learns a Lesson; Addy's Surprise; Happy Birthday, Addy; Addy Saves the
    Day;* and *Changes for Addy* by Connie Porter

Nettie's Trip South by Ann Turner

Answer Keys

Not All Southerners Were Slaveholders (page 7)
1. 75%

The Constitution: Many Compromises (page 9)
1. Possible answers include: violate, break, contravene, breach, transgress, disobey, encroach, impinge, trespass, intrude

Secession Divides the Nation: Part 2 (page 21)
1. The Confederate States were Alabama, Arkansas, Florida, Georgia, Louisiana, Mississippi, North Carolina, South Carolina, Tennessee, Texas, and Virginia.
2. The rest of the states remained with the Union.
3. Oklahoma
4. Washington, Dakota, Nebraska, Utah, Nevada, Colorado, and New Mexico

The Confederate Flag (page 25)
2. Stars, small stripe around the "X", and largest area: white
   Small square in left corner: red
   X-shaped area around the stars: dark blue

The War Begins (page 27)
3. Blockade: An attempt to force an enemy to surrender by preventing goods from reaching or leaving an area

Grant or Lee? (page 29)
1. Lee
2. Grant
3. Grant
4. Lee
5. Grant
6. Lee
7. Lee
8. Grant
9. Grant
10. Lee
11. Lee
12. Grant
13. Grant
14. Lee
15. Grant

Unpopular Decisions: Income Tax and the Draft (page 30)
3. $210.84
4. $512.30
5. $117.45
6. 0
7. $31.20
8. $731.40

What Did They Wear? (page 35)
Teacher check uniforms compared to key.

The Gettysburg Address (page 36)
1. 87 years
2. To dedicate the battlefield to those who died there
3. To ensure that those who died did not die in vain; to preserve the government dedicated to democracy

The First Air Corps (page 39)
1. Aerial: overhead; in the air
2. Surveillance: close watch; spying

What Did They Eat? (page 42)
A. grits
B. fatback
C. chitlins
D. cracklings
E. buttermilk
F. hush puppies
G. Johnnycakes
H. dodgers
I. Hoppin' John
J. okra
K. hog jowls
L. hardtack
M. salt pork
N. collard greens
O. cobbler
P. hog maws

Fact or Opinion? (page 47)

1.	O	6.	F
2.	F	7.	O
3.	F	8.	O
4.	O	9.	F
5.	O	10.	F

North or South? (page 49)

1.	S	9.	S
2.	N	10.	N
3.	S	11.	N
4.	N/S	12.	N
5.	S	13.	N
6.	N	14.	S
7.	S	15.	S
8.	S	16.	N

Scavenger Hunt (page 52)

1A. South Carolina
1B. Thomas Sumter, a Revolutionary War general
1C. Pentagon
2. James Buchanan
3. Traveller
4. *H.L. Hunley*
5. His name was accidently changed when the congressman who recommended him for West Point listed him as Ulysses Simpson Grant.
6. Simpson, Grant's mother's maiden name
7. Dozens of elephants
8. Hannibal Hamlin
9. Julia Ward Howe
10. P.G.T. Beauregard
11. Harriet Ross Tubman
12. John Brown

Order, Please (page 55)

A.	8
B.	4
C.	2
D.	10
E.	3
F.	7
G.	1
H.	6
I.	9
J.	5

True or False? (page 56)

1.	F
2.	T
3.	F
4.	F
5.	F
6.	T
7.	F
8.	T
9.	T
10.	T
11.	F
12.	T
13.	F
14.	F
15.	T